BIG
BIG DINOSAURS

by Catherine Ipcizade

Consulting Editor: Gail Saunders-Smith, PhD

Consultant: Jack Horner,
Curator of Paleontology
Museum of the Rockies
Bozeman, Montana

CAPSTONE PRESS
a capstone imprint

Pebble Plus is published by Capstone Press,
151 Good Counsel Drive, P.O. Box 669, Mankato, Minnesota 56002.
www.capstonepress.com

092009
005618CGS10

 Books published by Capstone Press are manufactured with paper
containing at least 10 percent post-consumer waste.

Library of Congress Cataloging-in-Publication Data
Ipcizade, Catherine.
    Big dinosaurs / by Catherine Ipcizade.
    p. cm. — (Pebble Plus. Big)
    Summary: "Simple text and photographs describe big dinosaurs" — Provided by publisher.
    Includes bibliographical references and index.
    ISBN 978-1-4296-3995-8 (lib. bdg.)
    1. Dinosaurs — Size — Juvenile literature. I. Title. II. Series.
QE861.5.I63 2010
567.9 — dc22   2009026042

Editorial credits
Erika L. Shores, editor; Ted Williams, designer; Wanda Winch, media researcher; Eric Manske, production specialist

Photo credits
Jon Hughes, cover, 5, 7, 9, 17
Picture Window Books/James Field, 1, 11; Steve Weston, 13, 15, 19, 21
Shutterstock/pinare, cover (background)

Note to Parents and Teachers

The Big set supports national science standards related to life science. This book describes
and illustrates big dinosaurs. The images support early readers in understanding the text. The
repetition of words and phrases helps early readers learn new words. This book also introduces
early readers to subject-specific vocabulary words, which are defined in the Glossary section.
Early readers may need assistance to read some words and to use the Table of Contents,
Glossary, Read More, Internet Sites, and Index sections of the book.

Table of Contents

Big

Big horns, teeth, and tails
helped dinosaurs stay alive.
Earth's biggest animals
first lived about 230 million
years ago.

Diplodocus was 90 feet
(27 meters) long.

Triceratops had a big head.

Horns stuck out above its eyes.

Triceratops also had

a horn on its nose.

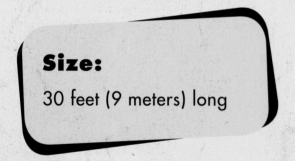

Size:

30 feet (9 meters) long

Tyrannosaurus rex had
big teeth to crush prey.
Each tooth was as long
as a banana.

Size:

46 feet (14 meters) long

Bigger

Giganotosaurus was

a big meat-eating dinosaur.

It stood 15 feet (5 meters) tall.

Size:

48 feet (14.6 meters) long

Spinosaurus had a big sail

on its back.

The sail was spines

covered with skin.

Size:

49 feet (15 meters) long

Biggest

Apatosaurus had a small head
and a big body.
It ate plants all day
to keep its stomach full.

Size:

90 feet (27 meters) long

Brachiosaurus was a big dinosaur that ate plants. It had a long neck to reach leaves on treetops.

Size:

92 feet (28 meters) long

Argentinosaurus shook
the ground when it walked.
This big dinosaur weighed
more than 10 elephants.

Size:

100 feet (30 meters) long

Seismosaurus was
the longest dinosaur.
It used its tail like a whip
to scare away other
big dinosaurs.

Size:

130 feet (40 meters) long

Glossary

horn — a hard, bony growth on the head of an animal

prey — an animal hunted by another animal for food

sail — a long row of spines covered with skin that stuck up on the back of Spinosaurus

spine — a sharp, stiff, pointed part of an animal

Read More

Johnson, Jinny. *Brachiosaurus and Other Dinosaur Giants.* Dinosaurs Alive! North Mankato, Minn.: Smart Apple Media, 2008.

Most, Bernard. *How Big Were the Dinosaurs?* Orlando, Fla.: Red Wagon Books, 2008.

Internet Sites

FactHound offers a safe, fun way to find Internet sites related to this book. All of the sites on FactHound have been researched by our staff.

Here's all you do:

Visit *www.facthound.com*

FactHound will fetch the best sites for you!

Index

Word Count: 153

Grade: 1

Early-Intervention Level: 12